THE MAJOR WORKS OF ERNEST HEMINGWAY

A CRITICAL COMMENTARY

STANLEY COOPERMAN
ASSOCIATE PROFESSOR OF ENGLISH
SIMON FRASER UNIVERSITY

MONARCH PRESS

NOTE:
THIS GUIDE IS INTENDED TO SUPPLEMENT AND ENHANCE,
AND IS NOT A SUBSTITUTE FOR, THE ORIGINAL WORK OF ART.

Copyright © 1964, 1965 by
SIMON & SCHUSTER, Inc.

All rights reserved. No part of this book may be reproduced in any form without permission in writing from the publisher.

Published by
MONARCH PRESS
a division of Simon & Schuster, Inc.
1 West 39th Street
New York, N.Y. 10018

Standard Book Number: 671-00621-5

Library of Congress Catalog Card Number: 65-7244

Printed in the United States of America

CONTENTS

Introduction	5
Biographical Sketch	10
A Critical Analysis of Four Novels	14
A Farewell to Arms	15
The Sun Also Rises	32
For Whom the Bell Tolls	42
The Old Man and the Sea	53
Survey of Critical Opinion of Ernest Hemingway	62
Bibliography	66

INTRODUCTION

There has been no American writer like Ernest Hemingway. Perhaps it might be more accurate to say that there has been no American like Ernest Hemingway who was also a writer. For this *enfant terrible* of the World War I "lost generation" was in many ways his own best character. Whether as the young "Champ" or as the middle-aged "Papa," Ernest Hemingway became a legend in his own lifetime. So completely has his name been absorbed into American culture, that he might almost seem a hero of folklore rather than a creative writer.

From New England campuses to Oregon lumber-camps, the name of Ernest Hemingway is known, and known well, even by men and women who find it difficult to remember when they last opened a book of serious literature. People who never read anything Hemingway wrote and cannot produce the title of one of his books will often know exactly what you mean by "the Hemingway type of man," and are more than likely to know something about "the Hemingway style." Whether Hemingway "belongs to the ages" certainly can be (and has been) debated. But there can be no doubt that he "belongs" to the people of America and the people of the world.

Although the drama and romance of his life sometimes seem to overshadow the substance of his work, the fact remains that Ernest Hemingway was first and foremost a literary man—a writer and reader of books. This is too easily forgotten amid all the talk about safaris and hunting trips, adventures with bullfighting, fishing, and war. That Hemingway enjoyed being famous is clear enough; he played in the public spotlight with enthusiasm. But he was also aware of the fact that any artist who makes "good news copy" is in danger of becoming little more than another Sunday-Supplement feature. And Ernest

Hemingway was an artist—a man who knew very well that a writer might become a "celebrity" for all the wrong reasons.

THE ARTIST. It was not enough for Ernest Hemingway to be a "celebrity." He was a writer and the job of the writer is to write. As a young man in Paris after World War I, he read voraciously and wrote deliberately with a kind of self-discipline approaching severity. Far from being the romantic soldier-of-fortune, the "lost" expatriate drifting from bar to bed to bullfighting arena, Hemingway, from the very beginning, was preoccupied with his craft, his art, his work. Literature was never far from his mind, so much so that Gertrude Stein once described him as being, despite his play-acting, a man of "museums"—an image which hardly fits the the Sunday-Supplement portrait of Hemingway the Bearded (or unbearded) Adventurer. In Paris, Hemingway himself recollected, "I was trying to write, and I found that my greatest difficulty (apart from knowing what you truly felt, rather than what you were supposed to feel, or what you had been taught to feel) was to note what really happened in action, what the actual things were which produced the emotion which you experienced. . . . I was trying to learn to write, commencing with the simplest things. . . ."

This preoccupation, which must be the preoccupation of any artist, never deserted Ernest Hemingway. In the lean years when his work was going badly, no amount of hunting or fishing or bullfighting could drown the taste of his own future—or fear of failure. "He had destroyed his talent by not using it, by betrayals of himself, by drinking so much . . . by laziness, sloth, and by snobbery, by pride," he says of the writer in *The Snows of Kilimanjaro,* adding that "the thought of his own death obsessed him. . . ." This was a warning that Ernest Hemingway gave to himself many times in his life, with an intense honesty basic to the man no less than to his work. "You made an attitude that you cared nothing for the work you used to do, now that you could no longer do it."

This would seem to be a peculiarly solemn self-reproach from a Romantic Adventurer—or perhaps not so peculiar after all. For Ernest Hemingway understood all too well that while many men can function in obscurity, it takes a strong man to survive his own fame—at least as an artist. In his brief message accepting the 1954 Nobel Prize, for example, Hemingway remarked that "a writer is driven far out past where he can go, out to where no one can help him." And in this acknowledgement of essential loneliness, the ever-present danger of failure which must accompany true work, Hemingway was reminding his public—and himself—that every artist must indeed be Santiago the fisherman in *The Old Man and the Sea;* that is, an individual who attempts to transcend his own limitations.

THE HEMINGWAY CULT. That Hemingway's work has limitations is obvious enough, and it is unfortunate that efforts to define these limitations have often aroused passions which have nothing to do with the work itself. Something of a "Hemingway cult" has arisen, a sort of club encouraged by men who often seem more like cheer-leaders than literary critics. Hemingway himself, of course, was partially responsible for this development; haunted by fear of failure all his life—failure of art, failure of nerve, failure of other and perhaps more intimate areas of existence—Hemingway could tolerate little criticism. Too often he reacted to challenges either with bellowing denunciation or adolescent sulking, and questioned the motives, not to mention the manhood, of those who actually cared enough to read his work instead of merely praising it. His use of baseball-boxing-hunting jargon in the most absurd circumstances indicated that Hemingway had come to believe in his own "colorful" public image; unleavened by self-perspective or self-humor, the mannerisms had become the substance. "I trained hard and I beat Mr. de Maupassant," he bombulated to Lillian Ross of *The New Yorker;* "I've fought two draws with Mr. Stendhal and I think I had an edge on the last one." Only Hemingway could have said it, and only Hemingway could have believed it.

It is always difficult, of course, to know when a writer's subject becomes an obsession, but Hemingway's insistence on "virility" and "manhood" does have its ludicrous aspects; and, one cannot escape the conclusion that his perpetual assertion had its basis in some murky sub-stratum of anxiety. Certainly, the Hemingway hero is often a refugee from what is ultimately the most "dangerous" area of existence: the complexities of the human soul. Action itself, after all, may be a narcotic—a way of making it unnecessary to "confront" any experience that cannot be handled as one handles a gun or a trout-line. It is possible for a man to be so frightened of life that he has to run out and shoot something, and in this sense Hemingway's work has been termed, with some justice, an "art of evasion."

LIMITATIONS. Throughout Hemingway's work there is a panic-stricken flight from all complexity, human or non-human, and this produces a thin aesthetic. It is one thing for an artist to translate complexity into simplicity; it is quite another thing to ignore the complexity altogether, and to limit one's work to those areas where "thinking" is no longer necessary. This reservation applies to his language as well. It may be true that, as Hemingway said, good prose is like an iceberg, with only a small part showing on the surface. But it is also true that icebergs must remain in chilly and arctic waters—or they turn to mush. If the "hard" surface of Hemingway's prose is in some ways admirable, in other ways it is the product of weakness rather than strength.

This is not to say that Hemingway's work is to be dismissed as insignificant. Indeed, it was precisely because Ernest Hemingway was an artist that he could turn his own failures, his own fears, into an art which is both significant and true. But in order to understand what he *did* produce, it is necessary to understand what he *could not* produce. In short, Hemingway made the best possible use of his limitations, but we must clearly define these limitations in order to appreciate the use to which he put them.

Two episodes in Hemingway's life—the fact that he was "blown up" in World War I, suffering a painful and terrible wound without any "stance of manhood" whatsoever, and the fact that his father committed suicide—shaped many of his attitudes, and indeed shaped much of his work. Like Frederic Henry in *A Farewell to Arms*, like Jake Barnes in *The Sun Also Rises*, like all of his heroes in all of his books, the fear of "thinking" and the fear of "letting go" was always close to Ernest Hemingway. The nightmare of chaos and passivity was a terrible nightmare, and one to be avoided, at all costs. That Hemingway evolved his own solutions to this nightmare, and based his art upon them, is something for which everyone interested in people and books must be thankful. But we need not assume that his solutions were universal ones, nor need we shrink from examining the art itself.

Each man exists in his own skull, and this is true of readers no less than of writers. Those critics who attempt to bully readers into awe-stricken admiration, who intimate that anything but praise of Hemingway is in some way tantamount to a failure of "virile imagination," do no service to Ernest Hemingway, and even less service to literature. The present book is an attempt to help readers *understand* Hemingway's work, and to perceive the weakness and strength which made this work possible. It is neither a tribute nor a confession of faith.

BIOGRAPHICAL SKETCH

Ernest Hemingway was born on July 21, 1899, in Oak Park Illinois, the second of six children. His father, Dr. Clarence E. Hemingway, a physician and enthusiastic outdoorsman, helped shape Hemingway's love for hunting and fishing. This influence was not unopposed by Hemingway's mother, Grace Hall Hemingway, who was a religious and pious woman; she wanted Ernest to learn music. But the young Hemingway followed his father's example; he spurned the church organ and took to the fishing rod and gun. Dr. Hemingway, however, despite his pursuit of outdoor sports, was rather sentimental and over-domesticated at home—a fact which the young Hemingway resented and remembered in later years.

At school Hemingway was a "loner" although he edited the school paper. Not especially popular, he learned through his school experience that life is hard, and that only the tough-minded survive. Hemingway's life at this time reflected his growing restlessness. He learned boxing and suffered a broken nose and serious eye injury; he ran away from home twice and spent months "on the road," working at a variety of jobs.

When the United States entered World War I in 1917, Hemingway tried to enlist, but was rejected because of his eye injury. After working as a cub reporter on the *Kansas City Star* he served as a volunteer ambulance driver in Italy where he was "blown up" by a mortar shell and received a wound which was to leave serious scars on his mind and spirit.

NEWSPAPERING. On his return to the United States, Hemingway worked as a newspaperman for the *Toronto Star and Star Weekly*. He came to know many good writers, among them

Sherwood Anderson. In 1921 he married Hadley Richardson and returned to Europe, getting to know and love Spain, Switzerland, Austria, and France. At the age of 23 he covered the Greek-Turkish war as a journalist; by the time he was 25 he had interviewed such world-famous figures as Lloyd George, Clemenceau, and Mussolini.

After covering the war Hemingway went to Paris with an introduction from Sherwood Anderson and met Gertrude Stein. He was seriously trying to write at this time but all was not going well with his marriage: Hadley was pregnant and wanted to return home. Meanwhile, Hemingway's stories had began appearing in avant-garde and popular magazines (including *Atlantic Monthly*). In 1923 he published *Three Stories and Ten Poems*; in 1924 *In Our Time*—a series of 32 fragments—was published in Paris. The collection of Nick Adams stories, *In Our Time*, was published in the United States the following year, and in 1926 *The Torrents of Spring* appeared, as did Hemingway's first successful novel, *The Sun Also Rises*.

Divorced from Hadley in 1927, Hemingway married—that same year—Pauline Pfeiffer, an editor of *Vogue*. In 1928 came a great shock: the suicide of his father, an event which affected him profoundly.

Later in 1928 Hemingway left Europe and took up residence at Key West, Florida, where Patrick Hemingway was born in 1929 and Gregory in 1932. *A Farewell to Arms*, which had appeared in 1929, sold 80,000 copies in four months and assured Hemingway of financial security. Hemingway now had three children (John Hemingway was the son of his first marriage), and was well into the role of "Papa."

In 1932 appeared *Death in the Afternoon*, and in 1933 *Winner Take Nothing*. During 1933 Hemingway also published the first of thirty-one articles and stories which were to appear in *Esquire* during the next six years.

Never one to stay put for long, Hemingway then traveled extensively, and the result was *The Green Hills of Africa* which appeared in 1935. With the outbreak of the Spanish Civil war in 1936, he devoted himself to the cause of the Loyalists, and in 1937 served in Spain as a correspondent for the North American Newspaper Alliance. That same year marked the appearance of *To Have and Have Not*—three related stories, two of which had been published separately. In 1938 Hemingway published *The Fifth Column and the First Forty-Nine Stories*—a volume containing the title play, and all the stories of his previous collections, in addition to seven published but uncollected tales.

TOWARD THE END. Hemingway completed *For Whom the Bell Tolls* in 1940, but his marriage was once again heading for the divorce court, and in 1940 he and Pauline separated. Hemingway promptly married the writer Martha Gelhorn (also in 1940), and began new travels with his new wife; after visiting China, they settled in Cuba. When World War II erupted, Hemingway leaped into the fray. After editing *Men at War* in 1942, he served as a war correspondent, accompanying American troops as they pushed the German forces back across Europe. Hemingway took to the war with enthusiasm; known as "Papa" by respectful troops, and a celebrity everywhere, he helped "liberate" the Ritz Hotel in Paris, actually posting a guard at the entrance with a notice: "Papa took good hotel. Plenty stuff in cellar."

Divorced from Martha in 1944, Hemingway had married Mary Welsh, a *Time Magazine* correspondent; after the war they settled in Venice. In 1950, *Across the River and Into the Trees* appeared, and met with much critical disapproval. This response infuriated Hemingway; *The Old Man and the Sea,* which appeared in 1952, was seen by some readers as an attack on the critical "sharks" themselves. Again Hemingway traveled, and in 1954 narrowly escaped death in an airplane crash, an event which occurred in the same year that he received the Nobel Prize. After a period of illness, Ernest Hemingway met his death as the victim of a "self-inflicted gunshot wound" in 1961, at Ketchum, Idaho, in the rugged country he loved so well.

A CRITICAL ANALYSIS OF FOUR NOVELS

In the following analysis, we shall examine the basic themes, ideas, and convictions Hemingway expresses in his work and some of the concepts in which these ideas are embodied. We shall first determine what these themes and concepts are and how they are used in *A Farewell to Arms,* and then continue to analyze their configuration in *The Sun Also Rises, For Whom the Bell Tolls,* and *The Old Man and the Sea.* Finally we shall note the elements of Hemingway's style and observe any differences of style among these novels.

I. A FAREWELL TO ARMS

THE HERO AND REALITY

The basic philosophical premises from which all of Hemingway's work proceeds are: that God does not exist, and that furthermore, there is not even such a thing as human nature. Thus there are no guidelines, no rules for life. As Sartre puts it, "Man is nothing but what he makes of himself." In the face of this conviction, man is lost in his world, forced to pick his way from moment to moment, to create his own rules for life. But life does not lend itself to individual solution without struggle, and ultimately man must face the fact that whatever he may make of his life, it will end in death. This is the reality which Hemingway's characters constantly confront and it is against the background of this reality that the characters and events of his novels must be viewed.

But to understand the full import of this background we must also understand what the nature of this "lostness" of man is. We can turn to Sartre for a further illumination of this idea when he refers to it as "forlornness," which, he says, follows when we understand that "God does not exist and we have to face all the consequences of this." This is very different from the simple idea of atheism, which holds that while God does not exist per se, the norms of honesty, progress and humanism can still be considered as having an *a priori* existence (ideas valid without proof). For Sartre, as for Hemingway, it is nowhere "written that the Good exists, that we must be honest, that we must not lie," and consequently, "man is forlorn, because neither within him nor without does he find anything to cling to."

GOD AND VALUE. Yet for Hemingway, as for his heroes, the fact that God is *not* does not obviate the matter of religion as a live concern. It would be a mistake to assume that the hard reality which Hemingway predicates as the precondition for existence means that the author is nihilistic. Sartre plumbs the importance of this distinction in terms of the existentialist, who, he says, "thinks it very distressing that God does not exist, because all possibility of finding values in a heaven of ideas disappears along with Him; there can no longer be an *a priori* Good, since there is no infinite and perfect consciousness to think it. . . . Indeed, everything is permissible if God does not exist." Thus while Hemingway's premises preclude both a divine and humanistic ideal as a standard of value and conduct, they do leave the field of life open to man, to "what he makes of himself."

Into this field of life Hemingway enters his hero, who exists first of all as a man who has learned—or comes to learn—this view of reality, and who, above all, confronts with full and steady cognizance the fact of death. But the hero's life does not merely constitute a despairing confrontation of man's impermanence. Rather, the state of man is taken as one of the preconditions with which the hero must come to terms in coming to terms with himself. And it is the *way* that the hero proceeds toward this coming to terms in which he identifies himself as one of the heroic, the elect. The way of the hero is not an abstract ideal, but a rule for life which the hero has made for himself, a rule which holds with various slight modifications for all Hemingway's heroes and which has generally been called the "Hemingway Code."

THE "HEMINGWAY CODE." In accordance with this code, the hero must establish his own values by facing life courageously and by acting honestly in terms of this reality. There is no alternative in life, and in fact those who seek alternatives find inner as well as outer distaster. Thus the primary attribute of the hero is courage. He does not turn from that reality toward any abstract ideal such as can be found in religion or politics. He does not pretend that people or situations are other than they are, no matter how inimical they might be to him. Further, he avoids the deceit of self-pity because it is a fundamental form of dishonesty. He knows that, in Hemingway's terms, we are all "biologically" trapped—that is, all men find themselves in the same condition merely by being born. Thus it is dishonest to pity oneself as if one's own lot were worse than another's. In terms of the ultimate reality, the condition of all men is the same: we are all part of a universe offering no assurance before or beyond the grave, and we must all make what we can of life in cognizance of that fact. There is an additional element of the heroic state which is consequent on this idea: the hero must not make trouble for others. (From this point of view we might say, in effect, that man is free, but his freedom only extends to the end of the next man's nose.) Finally, the hero must view others with as little moral condemnation as possible, not because he does not distinguish between good and bad, but because he tries to view other men objectively, with "irony and pity."

RULES AND MEANS. These are the ground rules by which Hemingway's hero stands or falls and against which each of his heros can be evaluated by the reader. But to understand the nature of the hero fully, we must also be aware of the *means* by which the hero seeks to maintain these rules in the face of the unrelenting conflict of life—the means are action and ritual.

Action—in their insistence upon it to the exclusion of all other approaches to life, Hemingway's heroes take their form. To the last, they are men who choose to act, to feel, to engage sensibly in the world about them rather than to observe or think about what is going on before them. Rather it means that they cannot choose to observe rather than act, and that they must distrust thought as a substitute for action. It is thought used as an *intellectual* approach to life that must be avoided, an attitude which reflects Hemingway's own distrust of the abstractions which intellect, unchecked by experience, can create. Thus action is a logical concomitant of honesty, because to Hemingway, action means experience of reality and thus avoids the unreality of unchecked ideas. It forces the hero to engage with objective reality which is the antithesis of subjective, and therefore possibly confusing ideas. His insistence on action as the hero's mode of life is also based on the idea that action is the means by which the hero can exercise his will, by which he can choose "what he makes of himself." An essential quality of Hemingway's work is consequently a fear of *otherness,* an avoidance of whatever cannot be controlled by will. The other, the *not-me,* is tolerable only insofar as it can be manipulated, as one manipulates a gun, a bull-fight, a load of dynamite, or a fishing line—as do the heroes of the four novels respectively.

ACTION AND PASSIVITY. In this context, action is also the antidote to what was for Hemingway the ultimate nightmare—male passivity. Hemingway's hero image is deeply enmeshed in the very idea of manhood itself, and thus passivity is an anathema, both because it means inaction and thus subjective thought, and because it constitutes the feminine rather than the masculine posture to life. Since Hemingway clearly views the feminine principle as one that is identified with nature, and thus in part with man's "biological" situation, its concomitant, passivity, is identified with yielding to that situation. This the hero must avoid, for thereby he would give up his control of his destiny and would be defeated. Thus man must be the doer rather than the person done-to; he must retain the initiative against the forces of life, against the unknown, against even death.

The role of death and the hero's involvement with it is one of the central themes of all Hemingway's novels, and one which has been much discussed and interpreted. To Hemingway, death is the ultimate reality, and thus it is the fact the hero must most surely confront. Consequently, all of Hemingway's heros in their confrontation with life are, in a sense, always in training for their confrontation with death. Yet, if the hero is not to be passive in this confrontation, he must control, and even choose his death. The task which Hemingway has set his hero is to *dominate* death: to overcome it, in a sense, by meeting it in the fullness of his hero-hood—with courage, with honesty, without self-pity, and with full awareness of its presence.

DESTRUCTION VS. DEFEAT. It is out of this idea that Hemingway's distinction between destruction and defeat arises. Destruction is death per se: the world ultimately breaks everyone, and death, as Dylan Thomas said, "shall have his dominion." But whether a man is *defeated* or not depends upon whether or not he dies spiritually—afraid, dishonestly appealing to God or attributing his death to some non-existent ideal, and with self-pity. The man who dies spiritually, whether he dies physically or not, is defeated. Thus man must dominate death by remaining undefeated, as the ideal soldier dominates in battle, as the bull-fighter dominates the bull, as the fisherman dominates the fish. And the way that Hemingway holds as the way to this domination is to see life as a ritual of action with certain rules which must be obeyed.

RITUAL, LIFE AND ART. Everything depends upon the necessity for ritual, even art itself. This is one reason why Hemingway's art seems so full of caution, deliberation, and wariness. Such qualities are not those usually associated with realistic writing—unless we understand that to Hemingway the need for ritual in life is no less vital than is the need for the careful construction of the feeling of reality in art; in fact, the construction is part of the ritual. For ritual is a means whereby man can control and thus dominate his actions. It is a bulwark against passivity—and in this sense, ritual has always been one of humanity's basic needs, whether it is in the temple, the bed, the arena, or on the battlefield. Thus we find that Hemingway's heroes are deeply involved in their own ritual. They choose their sphere of action from those which require ritual forms which they carefully follow; they are ritualistic in love and in death; and when they are confronted with their private rituals which, for the moment, push aside the dark. For the purpose of ritual is also to overcome fear—fear of the uncontrollable, the unknown, of death.

It is for this reason that the hero's relations with women are also surrounded by ritual. Women are also allied with the biological trap, and thus with the forces in the world that can reduce men to passivity. This does not mean that the hero cannot love a woman without falling from his heroic status, or that he does not desire a woman as other than a physical need. Rather it means that he must avoid being dominated by a woman, becoming her subject rather than her master; he must always retain his own identity and purpose in love.

THE NOVEL AND THE WAR

Against this background of Hemingway's view of reality and the purposes and demands upon the hero, we can approach the hero, his alternates, and the woman he loves in *A Farewell to Arms* with better understanding, and we can also comprehend more clearly what the central objective reality of the novel— The War—meant in terms of Hemingway's vision.

Frederic Henry typifies the thousands of young American men who, like Hemingway himself, volunteered for service in the "Great Crusade," as the rhetoric of the time called what more realistic, if not less metaphorical observers were to call the "circus of death." It was a Crusade to save *La Belle France* or "Classic Italy" or "Christian Civilization" from an enemy branded by a vast propaganda campaign as bestial and subhuman. But it was also a Crusade in which the young Americans expected to find "adventure," to prove their "manhood," and to taste martial glory and Noble Sacrifice. These slogans which echo so mockingly through the novel were created by a society that was still giving lip-service, if not credence, to the idea that a perhaps demanding but benevolent God did exist, and that there was such a thing as human nature—man as Rousseau had seen him—basically kind, honest, and loyal.

THE WAR OF THE MACHINE. But the Crusade stalled in the mud and blood of the war itself, and all the slogans, and the ideas from which they had been fashioned to justify the war were mired with it. For very few people—least of all the young volunteers themselves—understood that World War I was to be the first great war of the machine, the first war in which mechanics were far more important than heroes, and the first war in which unprecedented masses of men slaughtered each other with little or none of the "glory" or "test of manhood" that was supposed to be part of the military experience. Military leadership itself tended to be obsolete, and few generals had any clear idea of how to control either the machines or the masses of men at their disposal.

The result was a war in which individuals were reduced to helpless and hapless targets; a war in which both the brave soldier and the cowardly crawled about "from one bloody hole to another" and was likely to be killed—or not killed—quite by accident.

As a young boy in the Michigan north woods, Hemingway had learned to respect the strength and power of the individual creature—man or animal—alone with his own death. He had learned to respect courage and control, and had gone to war at the age of nineteen expecting an exercise in manhood. What he encountered seemed to be a ridiculous joke, except that there was nothing very funny about it. The real political reasons for the war, Hemingway and other young men of his generation were to discover, had little to do with the patriotic rhetoric and Noble Sentiments issued from the newspapers and pulpits of America. Even as a personal test of courage, the new kind of warfare was usually meaningless. It is certainly true that for Ernest Hemingway the shock of mechanized and impersonal warfare was even greater than the shock of political corruption. As early as 1922, for example, he wrote a short verse bitterly entitled *Camps d' honneur* ("Field of Honor") for *Poetry Magazine*:

> Soldiers never do die well:
>   Crosses mark their places—
> Wooden crosses where they fell,
>   Stuck above their faces.
> Soldiers pitch and cough and twitch—
>   All the world roars red and black;
> Soldiers smother in a ditch,
>   Choking through the whole attack.

Hemingway himself was wounded in World War I, under circumstances not unlike Frederic Henry's, and Hemingway was never to forget the absurdity of the circumstances: while he was engaged in nothing more "glorious" than handing out chocolates to Italian soldiers, a wandering shell ended his "adventure." Like Frederic Henry, his wound brought him up short before the absurdity of life ruled by accident. The new war of mud and machines was the dominant factor, obviating all ritual, taking the element of choice, of initiative, from the men who were engaged in it, making a mockery of personal courage. In Hemingway's terms the war became like the slaughter of animals in a stockyard, killing the good, the gentle and the brave with complete indifference.

THE "CIRCUS." Behind the "madhouse" theme that runs through so many novels of World War I is the fact that military leaders were not merely unprepared for mechanized war and vastly increased fire-power; they were also unprepared for the ideological revolution which provided them with unparalleled manpower. We must remember that before World War I, peacetime armies had been composed of a few gentlemen-professionals serving as officers, and enlisted men who represented the dregs of society. Very often a man would become a soldier in peacetime armies before World War I because there was nothing else he could do.

The armies of World War I, however, were composed of amateur soldiers, civilians drafted from all elements of the population. There were also volunteers who had embarked upon what they believed was a Crusade. Military leaders remained tragically unaware of the fact that methods of discipline appropriate for a limited army of social dregs could not be applied to mass armies representing all elements of the civilian population. And the application of such nineteenth-century concepts of discipline, combined with mass warfare and technological casualties, resulted in a vast increase in punitive executions or court-martials. On one hand the generals had very little notion of how to use their own fire-power efficiently; on the other, they tended to treat their own troops as cattle. Soldiers were there to die; that was their function. When any plan miscarried, when any offensive or retreat failed to take place according to schedule (Caporetto, for example), those soldiers who survived were by that very fact suspect. Hence Celine, the French novelist, remarks that the military administration "began to shoot troopers by squads, so as to improve their morale." In the face of this sort of logic, the hero, as a sane man caught in an insane machine of death, has only one choice: he must get out of it as best he can; the war he had originally come to fight has, in effect, "deserted him."

The chaos on the Italian front of *A Farewell to Arms* resembles the chaos elsewhere. By 1917, the Italians had lost almost one million men without any strategic gain whatsoever. Only a single important officer—a Colonel Douhet—dared to criticize the tactics of the Italian High Command, and he was court-martialed and imprisoned for his pains. The war had been reduced to a corpse factory, where the punitive executions reduced whatever remained of military duty to a final absurdity.

THE HERO AND THE HEROINE

The war thus constitutes the dominant expression of external reality in the novel, a reality which the reader is forced to participate in, not only through identification with the characters of the novel but through the medium of Hemingway's prose, in which language is used as if it were a camera, creating precise images of the noise, confusion, and slaughter. In the midst of this reality we can see that while Frederic Henry incorporates many of the characteristics of the Hemingway hero-ideal, he deviates in one important respect: he still seeks something beyond himself that he can look to—something "sacred"—and it is this that drives him on. While his honesty forces him to acknowledge in thought and action that service to the war, to a non-existent Crusade, is absurd, he is not completely able to face up to the fact that here is nothing that can justify life except living it. (Frederic Henry's very name is telling: it forces us to remember a figure similar in many respects—Patrick Henry, the American patriot who lived and died nobly, but did so for an abstract ideal, one which his partial namesake finds null and void in the era of mass warfare.)

We see Frederic's antithesis (in this respect only) in Rinaldi, to whom all "sacred objects" are suspect because he has learned all too well that people create them only when they can no longer face reality. Rinaldi shares the heroe's ethic in his awareness that there is "not a damned thing"—no God, no guiding principle—when he stops performing his personal ritual against the dark, his medical work. Yet he falls short of the ideal in that he makes trouble for others, baiting those who hold to ideas which differ from his views of reality and judging them harshly, in harsh words.

FREDERIC AND THE HERO. Yet in other respects Frederic is clearly identifiable as the type of the Hemingway hero. He is typical in that he distrusts verbal abstraction or even verbal sophistication. Anything that is "talked about" to any extent may be confused, it will be lost. Part of this refusal to place any faith in words is Frederic Henry's (and Hemingway's) scepticism about abstract values in general: patriotism, love honor, religion—all these things have been debased by a world which, under rhetorical verbiage, cheapens and falsifies the facts of life itself. As a reaction to such rhetoric, the "Hemingway Hero" limits his vocabulary to the concrete and exact, shuns any expression of emotion or sentiment, and often appears almost monosyllabic in his conversation.

Beneath this terseness, however, and beneath his insistence that reality is limited to that which can be killed, loved, measured, or tasted, Frederic Henry is a man of keen and almost romantic sensibilities. He is a man who expected much of the world, and has seen this expectation turn sour. The solution, of course, is to expect nothing at all—to live only in the immediate present. Once this is achieved, the individual can then enjoy whatever happiness does come his way; he can also endure, by an act of stoic will, whatever suffering is in store for him.

The important thing is never to whine, never to feel sorry for oneself, never to surrender to emotionalism and rhetoric. Life can only be endured if a man's will is maintained, if he *controls* himself and his environment. When the environment threatens to get out of control, a man must then try to discover another environment which *can* be controlled—hence the "Hemingway Hero" leaves war and turns to bullfighting, hunting, fishing, or making love. But all these must be done *cleanly,* and *exactly,* almost methodically. In a sense, the chief nightmare for Frederic Henry, as for other "Hemingway Heroes," is chaos, a situation where nothing is "clear" or "clean," so that a man can no longer exercise his will. Without will, a man is deprived of manhood itself.

This is a great fear, certainly. And so Frederic Henry deliberately limits both his loyalties and his definitions. Like all of

Hemingway's heroes, he wants to live without the complexities and convoluted definitions of abstract values. He wants to live in such a way as to maintain his own will, or manhood, by maintaining simplicity.

THE HEROINE. Frederic's ideal of simplicity is represented in the novel by Catherine Barkley; but to understand her particular role in the novel we must first take a brief look at the characteristics of Hemingway's women in general and the significance they hold as figures in his work.

First we must note that Hemingway's approach to his female characters is distinctly masculine. They are seen and valued in relation to the men in his stories and, insofar as they are purely feminine, he is not concerned with their inner world except as this world is related to the men with which they are concerned. Thus we see them primarily as love objects or as anti-love figures, a fact which has led many critics to view them as idealized and unconvincing, as the romantic vision of a youthful erotic daydream, too good (or bad) to be true. But if one is to appreciate and understand the women of the novels we are concerned with one must realize two things. One is that this kind of criticism is based on the standard of the naturalistic novel, and despite its surface appearances, Hemingway did not write—and did not intend to write—this kind of book. He was concerned with a more immediate reality than that which the accepted view of what was "natural" could present: the reality of what you *feel* when you see, not the scene you *think* you should see when you look. Secondly, Hemingway's heroines are not seen in a domestic world of kitchen sinks and tidied living rooms, or even in a world of conventional courtship. Rather, they exist in a heightened world accelerated by special events or circumstances. Nevertheless, they may consider a future home with their lover as a desirable possibility, and they often embody the image of home and create a sense of it in their environment.

FACE AND CHARACTER. In any case, Hemingway's heroines almost always embody the physical appearance of the ideal women in their striking beauty. But in their character they tend to appear as two types: the all-woman who gives herself entirely to the hero and the *femme fatale* who retains herself and in some way deprives the hero of possessing her completely. The all-woman is "good" in Hemingway's view because she submits her will and identity to the hero, wanting no other life than with him, no other man than he. By becoming subject to the hero, she allows him to dominate her and thus to assert his manhood. The *femme fatale* is always a more complex character than the good all-woman, and while she may or may not be a bitch, she does not submit to the hero and she wounds him and all the men who enter her sphere primarily because they cannot dominate her and thus cannot assert their manhood through her.

WOMAN AS GODDESS. But underneath the individuality of each heroine there runs an undercurrent of paganism, of a connection with the earth, with nature, which marks them as the personifications of what an earlier generation termed the "feminine principle." They are not Christians; they deny formal religion, believing more in such relics of pagan belief as fortune telling and good-luck charms. And in fact, in each novel they are identified as a kind of pagan deity—a witch, a goddess or a combination of both—allied with the primitive element in man. The identification in the novels is usually verbalized in no uncertain terms, but the terms are usually humorous. Nevertheless, the identification of their pagan aspect is valid and is re-enforced throughout the novel by incidents and images which restate the idea in various terms. Her goddess quality can also vary: she may represent the perfection and yielding sensual femininity of Aphrodite or the cool beauty of an Athena; she may reflect the image of Helen of Troy—perfect in beauty and infinitely desirable, but bringing disaster to the men who fall in love with her; or, she may appear in the likeness of Hecate, the dark goddess of death and destruction; and finally she may appear as a mixture of several of these—as we shall see when we discuss *The Sun Also Rises*.

Yet despite Hemingway's tendency to use women as foils for his men, he characteristically makes them members of the elect. The heroine, like the hero, obeys the "Hemingway Code." She sees life for what it is even as she longs for something more certain; she is courageous in life, choosing reality over abstractions; and she faces death stoically. But in each case there has already been in her life some tragic event—the loss of a lover, violence—which presumably has given her the insight and experience which makes her able to face life this way.

CATHERINE BARKLEY. Catherine Barkley in *A Farewell to Arms* is clearly established in her goddess qualities—at first as a kind of Athena, beautiful, cool, and somewhat distant, and then as the yielding Aphrodite, the goddess who is concerned only with love and its expression. She also typifies Hemingway's "good" all-woman who gives herself completely to the hero and enables him to reaffirm his manhood through his love of her. Yet her goddess aspect penetrates even her all-woman role insofar as the hero elevates her to the status of a sacred object, an ideal that gives purpose to life. Nevertheless she holds to the harsh realities of the Hemingway Code, finding her meaning in her immediate world, denying formal religion as a source of comfort, and facing both her life and death stoically, with courage, and completely without self-pity. In her goodness and constancy to Frederic she has been criticized as a dream image, as a bland creature with very little personality, and as an unrealistic image of woman, even as the mountain love-interlude of Frederic and Catherine has been considered dreamlike and unreal. But in addition to what has been said earlier with regard to this criticism, we must note that the love affair of the novel takes place under extreme pressure, not in an everyday environment. The passionate relationship of lovers under stress is bound to be different from that of lovers who exist in what we consider normal circumstances. Under the pressure in which the love affair of the novel is conducted, the lovers are forced to abandon their everyday duties and responsibilities and to live only for each other. In the novel, the situation is the war gone wild and the pressure is the lovers' sense of the imminent doom at their heels which casts a shadow on their future.

In Frederic's relationship with Catherine, we can also see the hero in terms of Hemingway's Code with regard to women. In the beginning of their affair, Frederic is the embodiment of the hero free of woman, conducting the ritual of the love game with the control he might use in a game of chess. But once he elevates Catherine to the status of a sacred object he no longer adheres to the Code in this respect, becoming a man *not* free of woman. Yet, insofar as Catherine is passive and allows herself to be dominated by him despite his dependence on her presence, he remains within the boundaries of the Code. Thus it can be seen that the "Hemingway Code," like all strict rules for life, cannot be taken literally, even in the analysis of literature. We use them here as a sort of general standard, even as Hemingway did, to provide some measure against which we can evaluate his characters. But like real people, they will defy final, tidy analysis.

THE MOUNTAIN AND THE PLAIN. Finally we note that *A Farewell to Arms,* like many of Hemingway's works, incorporates an underlying symbolism which is found in the distinctions made between the connotations associated with the mountains and the plain. The mountains represent those virtues to which man aspires but which he can only have for a time; ultimately, all of Hemingway's heroes must descend again to the plain. Like the priest's mountain village in the novel, life in the mountains is simple and pure: it is peaceful and quiet, the people live with dignity in health and happiness, and the hunting—a hero's sport because in it he can take the initiative—is good. The mountains are also associated with pure air, which is also clear and dry. In contrast lies the plain, which in *A Farewell to Arms* is the arena for the war and for death. It is associated with suffering and disease, with indignity and defeat (using the word in the sense we have discussed). It is also associated with the rain, and rain in the novel is most often the prelude or the accompaniment to disaster. Carlos Baker has developed the distinction between mountain and plain to a fine point. He has extended it to include worship, or at least consciousness of God as an aspect of the mountains and irreligion as an aspect of the plains—ideas which provide another viewpoint from which the reader's understanding of Hemingway's work can be enriched. However, it is again necessary to note that the distinction should not be taken too literally. It is enough to understand that Hemingway makes skillful use of both weather and scenery to match the tone of his dramatic scenes.

REVIEW QUESTIONS: A FAREWELL TO ARMS

1. Discuss "verbal scepticism" in relation to the narrative of *A Farewell to Arms*.

ANSWER: "Verbal scepticism" refers to the distrust felt by such a man as Frederic Henry with regard to rhetoric or sentimentality. Because the Crusade of World War I was accompanied by an extreme outpouring of rhetorical propaganda, a reaction set in against all abstractions. The result was a vocabulary deliberately limited to concrete words, things, actions, with as few abstractions as possible. As expression, this can be termed "understatement"—which means a deliberate attempt to limit the statement of emotion. For men like Frederic Henry, phrases such as "morality," "patriotism," "love," and "civilization" were too vague for any real meaning. Instead of such words, they depended on actions, or things-in-themselves. In *A Farewell to Arms* the understated narrative of Frederic Henry demonstrates both the advantages and disadvantages of the method; the narrative is clear, precise, honest. There is no attempt to "gush" over suffering or love. On the other hand, there is a certain quality of monotone which is not always effective, especially in long passages of dialogue.

2. Why is Hemingway's style often termed "the art of the unsaid"?

ANSWER: Because the Hemingway hero distrusts the rhetoric of emotion or sentiment, he avoids the direct statement of either. But beneath the monotone of his talk, like a face beneath a mask, may be a very deep and very real emotion. In fact, the deeper the emotion, the less it is verbalized. For men like Frederic Henry, the true emotions can only be "spoiled" if a man talks about them. Words have no validity in themselves. Instead of "talking," a man acts. He doesn't "talk" about bravery, for example, but proves it by action, and the same is true for love of a woman. Even in moments of fear or horror, the Hemingway hero may produce only a "deadpan" listing of facts; the facts themselves will produce the emotion for the reader, without additional help from mere words. In short: the Hemingway hero (or narrator) doesn't talk "about" emotion; he simply gives us the facts which produced it. And we must then "get" this emotion for ourselves.

3. Discuss two basic symbols in *A Farewell to Arms*.

ANSWER: Two basic symbols in *A Farewell to Arms* can be identified as rain-and-the-low-country on one hand, and snow-and-the-mountains on the other. The rain represents evil, defeat, complexity, corruption, uncleanliness. The chaos of war is associated with the rain; death waits in the rain. The mountains, however, represent clarity, order, cleanliness, purity, in contrast to the butchery of war on the plains.

II. THE SUN ALSO RISES

The basic setting for *The Sun Also Rises* is the permanent, self-renewing earth on which man is a transient, hemmed in by a birth he did not choose and a death toward which he must inexorably move. This basic juxtaposition is stated in the passage from *Ecclesiastes* from which the book takes its name: "One generation passeth away, and another generation cometh; but the earth abideth forever. . . . The sun also ariseth, and the sun goeth down, and hasteth to the place whence he arose," as eternal as the wind that returns "according to its circuit," and the rivers that return from "whence the rivers come." But the novel, like all of Hemingway's works, is not merely a despairing cry for man's impermanence. Rather the state of man is taken as the precondition of his life, and that with which man as the hero must come to terms. But death, in all its forms, is not all that man must deal with, for he must also engage with the rest of humanity which, like him, is struggling with its own condition. For if man's struggle is not to be entirely solitary, he must also have the company of other human beings. Yet while he desires and needs their company—and their communion—he must also contend with their conflicts, their desires, and with the feelings that they, in turn, elicit from him. And finally there is man's confrontation with the consequences of the struggle that has gone on before him, the struggle that we record as history.

PEOPLE, LAND, AND WAR. Thus in *The Sun Also Rises* we have the background of the land, and the river, and (as in *A Farewell to Arms*) we have the mountain and the plain; we have the people of the story who represent many kinds of approaches to life; and we have the First World War, which has established certain basic considerations of their existence.

The War is not present in the novel as it was in *A Farewell to*

Arms, for here we are concerned with its aftermath. But although it is only mentioned directly a few times in the novel, it is ever-present in the power of its effect upon the individuals who people the book. All the characters are suffering because of the war, directly or indirectly: Jake Barnes has been made sexually impotent; Lady Brett Ashley has lost her "true love"; and Cohn is unable to relate to those who have passed through the conflict. Those who have been immediately involved go through the most anguish and rely upon each other for support. Those who have been less involved are separated from the former by this lack of experience. There is an implied dilemma in Cohn's maladjustment: we can see him as a man who has been unable to mature because of his lack of war experience; with the war experience he might have been as disillusioned as Jake Barnes.

But above all, The War is implicit in the characters' approach to life, which is, for most of them, that predicated by the Hemingway Code. For the terribleness of The War, and the exposure of the moral dissolution of society that it brought about, seemed to Hemingway's generation to expose the ideals of society as illusions. Having nothing, no code, no belief which would serve in the stead of these ideas, the post-war generation found itself morally afloat. This is the meaning of "the lost generation" in Hemingway's novel: not the generation that is lost in the sense that it is ruined, but the generation that is unable to find a way of order for itself.

A HEROIC PROPORTION. Thus the characters are not merely portrayals of reckless, profane and dissipated people, as they have been viewed by some critics. Instead they constitute a kind of modern version of original man, man starting again from scratch. As such, they assume a certain heroic proportion, and as such they are bound to fall far short of any recognizable ideal. What is heroic about the characters in the novel is the extent to which they try to establish, each for himself, some mode of existence which fulfills their own *vision* of good. In fact, the book is divided between those characters—like Jake Barnes—who have the courage, first, to see that they are forlorn, and second to struggle to achieve a way of life that is honorable in the midst of their forlornness, and the characters—like Robert Cohn—who do not have the courage, who live in illusion and act upon it. The rightness of Hemingway's Code is also the thesis of the book. Jake Barnes, Bill Gorton, and Pedro Romero hold to the Code and they do not wreak destruction upon others. They are able to work, to create, and to remain independent and responsible. Robert Cohn, and to a lesser degree, Mike Campbell, do not hold to the Code; they hurt others and live like dependent children on the bounties of their families.

THE HERO WITH THREE FACES. The ideal of the hero is closely approximated in the book by three characters: the central character, Jake Barnes, his friend and sort of alter-ego Bill Gorton, and the hero in action, Pedro Romero. Jake is the hero who most clearly approaches the ideal of courage in his conscious personal confrontation with the unknown, the man who does not turn from the harshness of the reality he lives with despite the fact that he must live out his life under circumstances which would drive less courageous men to find some measure of support in an abstract ideal. He also embodies the other characteristics of the hero: the avoidance of self-pity and of making trouble for others, and an outlook toward other human beings which is generally without judgment and is based mostly on "irony and pity." He also shares Sartre's regret for the absence of God without allowing himself to be deluded into the emotion of actual worship. Jake, as well as the other heroic characters in the book—which include, as we shall see, the *aficionados*—are also characterized by the fact that they can recognize and establish an immediate understanding with another member of the breed. While this aspect of the elect appears in all of Hemingway's novels, it is especially emphasized in *The Sun Also Rises,* even to the extent that it is verbally acknowledged—by Brett, in particular.

THE ANTI-HERO. All the characteristics of the hero are emphasized in the novel through his antithesis, the anti-hero, Robert Cohn. The anti-hero bases his life on false ideas and ideals; he does not live by action, but by words, even by that least trustworthy source of words, romantic fiction; he is cowardly in spirit and full of self-pity; through his failure to see reality he is constantly making trouble for others; and finally, he is a man dependent on woman. Cohn fulfills this image. Remembering the bookish basis of Cohn's ideal man, it is likely that Hemingway also intended to imply that Cohn's vision of masculinity was identified with sexual virility, and that for him the proof of manhood lay in the proof of potency. While this attitude characterizes a well-known psychological type, what we are concerned with here is that this misapprehension of the nature of virility—which for Hemingway lies in courage, not merely potency—typifies the Hemingway *anti*-hero, not the hero himself. Hemingway has underlined this distinction clearly in creating Jake Barnes.

In contrast to Robert Cohn, Bill Gorton stands as another embodiment of the hero, a sort of quiet, less sharply seen reflection of a Jake Barnes with his sexual potency intact. He too, we gradually realize, despairs of making sense out of life, but he goes on to make the best of it without complaint. Instead of finding everything bitter, he calls everything "just wonderful"— in a world in which life, in Hemingway's own words, is a "damn tragedy," every place is substantially the same. At first the reader may take him at his word, but after his description of the attack on the Negro prizefighter in Vienna, we realize its meaning—or meaninglessness. Bill's membership among the heroic is also underlined in his ability to communicate wordlessly with Jake and the others of his kind.

THE HEROINE. Like all of Hemingway's heroines, Brett contains elements of a pagan deity. She is identified with Circe, the goddess "who turns men into swine," but she also reflects the characteristics of Helen of Troy as we viewed them in the previous chapter. Brett is thus both dark and light. She is unquestionably allied with the primitive forces in man, so that it is inevitable that she will come together with Romero who deals with these forces in the form of the bulls. But there is more to Brett than myth and symbol, and in terms of the Code she is raised above the dangerous and magical depths of her womanhood. Her virtues are those of the Hemingway ethic, except that she is, until the end, at the mercy of her desire. The ritual which she practices to still her inner anguish is not private, but requires another for its execution, and thus she injures others. But in the end, Brett's qualities are manifest in a heroic act, when she sends Romero away realizing that she could do nothing but lead him to emotional and professional ruin. Nevertheless, for her membership among the elect despite the fact that she is not one of Hemingway's "good" women, she pays a high price: although she bears a likeness to Helen of Troy whose "face launched a thousand ships," Hemingway repeatedly implies that she is, in many respects, masculine, and fears feminization.

THE BULLFIGHT. The novel's central expression of the heroic act lies in the bullfights, which to Hemingway epitomize the hero's chosen confrontation with death under the protection of ritual. In this setting, the bull represents death—not merely in the simple sense of an end to life, but death as an aspect of all the dark, powerful forces of nature which are at once the source of all life's energy and the means of its destruction. Untransformed, unconquered, untamed, the bull is dangerous, as is the untransformed, uncontrolled bull in man. But in conquering the bull within, man reaches his greatest heights, for then he can combine the great power of the bull with the clear vision of his consciousness to become a kind of super-man.

This idea and its enactment underlay the ancient bull cults which were once to be found around the world, and it is from their rituals that what we know today as the bullfight has descended in direct line. In reflection of its religious, mystical origins, the bullfight involves the element of transference,—the notion that the matador's engagement with the bull is *shared* by the spectators. Drawn in emotionally by the hypnotic beauty of the true matador's movements and the bull's response, the people become one with the matador. They too, confront death and kill the bull, while at the same time, they give the matador their combined strength, and it is with their power together with his dedicated skill that the deed is done.

THE *AFICIONADO* AND THE CODE. Understanding these unspoken elements, we can see the importance of the bullfight in the novel in terms of the Hemingway Code. The bullfight represents the ideal of action as a chosen confrontation with death, a confrontation in which the hero can achieve domination, both through the control provided by a carefully prescribed ritual and through courage. Further, the element of transference enables the hero to participate as a spectator—but only if, like Jake and Romero, he is a true *aficionado*.

The idea of the *aficionado* is important in the novel, for the *aficionado,* as Hemingway explains, is one who is *passionate* about bullfights. Like the heroic impulse with which it is identified, this passion forms a bond of understanding among its adherents. As Hemingway, in the novel, describes the way this bond is made manifest, we find that we are in the presence of something that has the quality of mystic ritual, including the sacred touch, or blessing, which so many religious rituals have in common. Hemingway also indicates his awareness of the origin of the bullfight—his descriptions of the community of *aficionados* imply a kind of membership in a bull cult presided over by Montoya as high priest. In the light of Montoya's complete acceptance of Jake as a member, or an initiate in this cult, the importance of his rejection of Jake as an accomplice in the union of Brett and Romero can be understood.

THE HERO AS MATADOR. Pedro Romero is the very epitome of the Hemingway hero both in the bull ring and out of it. Yet for the reader, he may not seem to be more than Jake, whose courage is maintained in the face of profound personal disillusionment as well as physical disability. Romero is uncorrupted by the mood of "the lost generation," and he has none of the anguish which besets the modern man of the wasteland—Jake and his party. As the critic Melvin Blackman notes: "With the instinctive sureness of a primitive who need never question his reason for living, he pursued his natural course . . . There was an absolute center to him."

Finally we have in the novel the distinction between the mountain and the plain, the rain and the sun. The plain in *The Sun Also Rises* is the plain on which the wasteland—of the city of Paris—pleasant, yet barren—is located, where the forlorn modern man finds his natural element. High in the mountains there is an atmosphere of purity, of simplicity, in which modern man can live in uncomplicated male companionship and engage in immediate action. Between these two lies the town of Pamplona, with a foot in both worlds.

A VIEW OF THE ENDING. The closing lines of the novel are often quoted to support the idea that the action as well as the background of the novel is cyclical, ending as it began. But while it is true that these lines superficially reflect the first exchange between Jake and Brett in the story, there is a great difference, both in the tone and in the meaning of the words. We can see in them the distance that Brett has come from the time when Jake's touch would turn her "all to jelly." And in a like manner, Jake has changed. This does not presuppose that Brett, Jake, or any of the other characters will change their mode of existence or find freedom from despair. Rather it reflects the idea discussed in the previous chapter: that the hero struggles constantly to confront the truth and to live by it, and to derive from his struggle a measure of value by which he can live still more honestly.

Nevertheless, the book is a tragedy because even the greatest courage does not enable the characters to rise above their circumstances, but only enables them to learn "how to live in it." That is the best Hemingway's hero can do in the face of a bitter reality, and the best is what Jake and Brett and Bill Gorton have done.

REVIEW QUESTIONS: *THE SUN ALSO RISES*

1. Relate the impact of World War I to the "Hemingway Code" as exemplified by Jake Barnes.

ANSWER: One of the major results of World War I—"The Great Crusade"—was the fact that many young people, especially those in literature and the arts, turned against the abstract "principles" and values of the older generation; it was the older generation, after all, that had created the war in the name of Patriotism, Glory, and the assorted Virtues. Young people insisted that whatever values an individual could hold for himself, had to be based on reality and truth. If life were harsh, the answers to the problems of life would have to cope with rather than avoid such harshness. Young people wanted an end to "illusion"—meaning the illusions of sentiment and rhetoric. And if, given the truth of the real world, no solutions were possible, a man could at least "lose with honor." He would redeem his own manhood by will, pride, and endurance: he would have the will to dominate what is possible, the endurance to suffer what he must, and the pride of knowing that he "acts well" even in the face of futility itself. In any event, he would neither whine nor make an emotional spectacle of himself.

Such is the "Hemingway Code" as exemplified by Jake Barnes —who typifies the man who faces his personal reality, contains his own suffering by the exercise of will, and imposes some meaning on a meaningless universe by his ability to achieve form through ritual—the "right" sort of personal action—and is able to maintain his *essential* manhood despite the reality he confronts.

2. Pedro Romero exemplifies one of "the great ones" as a matador, and the qualities which make him great as a bullfighter are those qualities which Hemingway insists must belong to any artist—including the literary artist. Discuss these qualities, and explain how they can be applied to the writer.

ANSWER: Like Pedro Romero, the artist is "true" and "pure" in his art. He does not strive to make his work "look hard"; on the contrary, his graceful writing is deceptively simple, easy, and exact. There are no false flourishes to call attention to themselves, and no attempt either to please the audience by overdramatic verbal "gestures." Like Romero's attitude toward his work, the artist is both intense and objective; he is able to judge his work dispassionately, as though it were something quite apart from himself. One might say that like Romero, the artist permits himself to be absorbed into the ritual of his art, and does not force the ritual into his own ego; his desires and fears are in a sense redeemed and transformed by the "purity" of the ritual itself. But this objectivity is not really simple at all, and neither is it "natural"; maintenance of ritual truth demands an enormous—though controlled—exercise of will, which in turn is based upon pride and endurance: a refusal to compromise with untruth or to rationalize weakness.

These qualities—simplicity, truth, precision, grace, and uncompromising honesty—are essential to the literary artist, as contrasted with the literary hack. The good writer, like the good matador, "stands alone" before failure; he confronts reality "cleanly," depending upon nothing but his own perception and timing. Just as the matador may "spoil" his performance, for example, by demanding too much aid from his assistants or by working with an overly weakened bull, so too the writer may spoil his art by propping it up with irrelevant problems or ready-made labels. In short, while the discussions of bullfighting in *The Sun Also Rises* are valuable in themselves over and above these descriptions, the definition of "the true matador" is in effect a statement of Hemingway's personal aesthetic creed.

3. Many critics have insisted that "right action" for the Hemingway hero is actually a form of protection against suffering, and for this reason (say the critics), Hemingway's work often demonstrates "narcotic action." Discuss those aspects of this idea that are relevant to *The Sun Also Rises*.

ANSWER: Stripped of all ready-made solutions to the problem of futility, the Hemingway hero might be compared to a man walking a tightrope: if he stops too long and begins "thinking," he is likely to lose his balance and fall. And so he tries not to stop—or think—at all; as long as he can keep moving, he can at least maintain his balance gracefully. The hero comes closest to losing his self-control at those moments when there is no clear pattern of action to help him contain his despair, a despair which is always close to the surface of his apparent stoicism. Night, for example, is a "bad time," because an individual's will is most relaxed and he is most likely to confuse or delude himself by "thinking."

Action—some form of ritual—is necessary not simply for aesthetic reasons, but also as a form of spiritual medication or insulation. Highly organized rituals such as the bull-fight or fishing provide one form of such "narcotic action," and when these are not available, a ritual can be made even of small things. Sometimes the hero will even try to steady his mind by looking carefully at external objects—details of a street or a room. Such action is used as a buffer ("narcotic") against his own suffering; it deadens his spiritual pain.

III. FOR WHOM THE BELL TOLLS

In December 1934, about six years before he completed *For Whom the Bell Tolls* and about two years before the outbreak of the Spanish Civil War, Ernest Hemingway warned that writers who use politics as an "easy way" to success are cheating themselves and their readers. "A writer can make himself a career while he is alive," said Hemingway, "by espousing a political cause, working for it, making a profession of believing in it, and if it wins he will be very well placed":

> "A man can be a Fascist or a Communist and if his outfit gets in he can get to be an Ambassador, or have a million copies of books printed by the government, or any of the other rewards the boys dream about. . . . But none of this will help him as a writer unless he finds something new to add to human knowledge while he is writing."

POLITICS AND ART. Hemingway was reminding his readers of a simple truth that we are likely to forget in any time of crisis: the fact that the writer, if he is to be a writer instead of a paid propagandist, must "choose up sides" not for any political creed, but for humanity itself. It took some courage for Hemingway to make this statement in 1934, when prevailing intellectual opinion in the United States (as elsewhere) was exerting pressure on the individual writer to demonstrate his "social responsibility." The experience of the great depression had made art-for-the-sake-of-art seem like a luxury, and the alienation of the "lost" generation seemed, in retrospect, a posture that nobody could afford. The good writer, it was felt, had to demonstrate that he was also a good citizen.

Hemingway himself, of course, understood that the writer could not work isolated from the crucial problems of his time. But he also understood that political dogma often fails to give a true insight into human problems and human motivations. Dogma, indeed, often obscures the truth it pretends to reveal—and the job of the writer, especially the socially responsible writer, is to recreate the whole truth to the best of his ability, including those aspects of the truth which the dogmatist prefers to ignore when it suits his purpose to do so. Hemingway—true to his creed as a literary artist—insisted upon presenting the entire truth as he saw it, and this he did with *For Whom the Bell Tolls.*

THE SPANISH CIVIL WAR. Because *For Whom the Bell Tolls* does represent at least a limited change in the work of Ernest Hemingway from political withdrawal to political commitment, it is necessary to understand something about the conflict which crystalized his decision to "come back from the bull-fight." This event was the Spanish Civil War of 1936-1939. It was a cruel war, and—from the ideological point of view—an extremely complicated one. For by the time the Civil War itself came to an end with the victory of General Franco's Fascist forces, it was obvious that greater issues were at stake than the government of Spain alone.

For almost a decade it had been obvious to astute political observers that the Nazism of Germany and the Fascism of Italy had been growing in power, arrogance, and efficiency, and that it was only a matter of time before they collided with the Communist power of Soviet Russia. The Spanish War provided both a testing ground and overture for World War II, when the dictatorships of the right and of the left engaged in a death struggle, and the western democracies were forced to leave their precarious neutrality and enter the conflict on a global scale.

During the Spanish Civil War, however, the western democracies refused to be involved, despite the fact that both Germany and Italy were obviously flexing their muscles on behalf of the Spanish Fascist rebellion. Desperately trying to protect their Republican government (which had ended the "royal dictatorship" of Alfonso XIII), the Republicans turned toward the left, and the struggle which had begun as an attempt to reform Spain's semi-feudal society took on the nature of a war-by-proxy between the two major radical movements of Europe: Communism and Fascism.

Imbued with a love for democratic ideals, and a hatred of Fascist tyranny, many young idealists from the western democratic nations supported the Republican cause in Spain. Faced with the fact that the democracies had washed their hands of the entire conflict, these idealists came to the conclusion that they had no choice but to work (and sometimes to fight) alongside the Communists, who were in effect the only allies of the Republican cause. Not all of these young men were themselves Communist; Robert Jordan, as we shall see, clearly indicates that he is in Spain not because he is a Communist, but because he hates Fascism. And the same was historically true of many young idealists of whom Robert Jordan is a dramatic representation.

DISILLUSION. George Orwell, for example (who was later to earn literary fame with his anti-Communist novel, *1984*), actually volunteered to serve with the Republican forces; his subsequent disillusionment is admirably recorded in *Homage to Catalonia,* a literary memoir that recreates a situation in which all ideological clarity seemed to have vanished in a mire of conflicting evils. The idealism, the bravery, and the ironic pathos of Robert Jordan—and the thousands of real-life Robert Jordans—certainly would be clarified for any reader of Hemingway's novel by a study of Orwell's non-fiction account of what is essentially the same sort of experience.

The actual sequence of events leading up to and including the Civil War may be briefly summed up as follows: Republican pressures against the reign of Alfonso XIII finally forced the monarch to call new elections in 1931. The result was overwhelming victory for Republican-Socialist coalitions, a victory so complete that Alfonso abdicated his throne, and the rule of monarchy—already weakened by rebellion in Africa and class conflicts in Spain itself—came to an end. The Republican government then attempted to establish reform in Spain, adopting a new constitution and proclaiming such basic tenets of democracy as religious freedom and the complete separation of Church and State.

But the government had to maintain a difficult balance between conservative groups (the Church, the army, and the landed aristocracy), and the more radical groups who drew their support from the workers and peasants. While the conservatives opposed virtually all liberal legislation, the leftists attacked the government for being too slow and cautious in providing it. Army officers revolted in 1932; radical uprisings took place in 1933; strikes paralyzed the economy in 1934. It was obvious that political power was being polarized toward the right and toward the left.

THE PROGRESS OF WAR. A coalition of Republicans, Syndicalists, Socialists, and Communists organized a "popular front" for the elections of 1936, and the result was an electoral triumph for the left. The government began immediate implementation of reforms, including the distribution of land, and there was some attempt to purge army officers who were loyal to the old aristocracy. Ideological differences among the various elements of the coalition, however, weakened the government, and when several army garrisons revolted on July 18, 1936, under the leadership of Emilio Mola and General Franco, the Spanish Civil War had begun.

The actual issue of the war was seldom in doubt. Military power was on the side of Franco's forces, who—in addition to their professional training—were aided by German and Italian equipment, ammunition, and men. The Fascist powers took the Civil War as a sort of laboratory; it was a chance to test their weapons—especially air weapons—in actual battle conditions, against flesh-and-blood targets. By the time the Republicans surrendered (in March, 1939), they had suffered about 800,000 dead in combat, in air-raids (which also hit civilian populations), and in a ruthless program of political execution.

For Ernest Hemingway, the events in Spain were intensely moving. Spain had long been his "favorite"—and the cities of Spain had come to occupy a place in his affections second only to Paris. The Spanish people, furthermore, with their intense individualism, their love of blood-rituals (such as the bullfight), their pride, and their semi-primitive alienation from the modern commercial world, had been "his" people. And when the Civil War made of this people mere pawns in an international struggle, Hemingway could not stand by uninvolved. He had to take part in some way. He had to "be there," and as a working newspaperman he actually was able to cover several major battles.

HEMINGWAY AND THE LOYALISTS. Hemingway's sympathies, of course, were bitterly anti-Fascist on emotional as well as intellectual grounds. "His" people were the peasants and the "true people" of the arena and the countryside; it was these groups who provided the most implacable foes of the Franco rebellion. Fascism, furthermore, was organized tyranny—a monolithic instrument for subduing individual freedom—and it was the organization no less than the tyranny which outraged Hemingway. Finally, the Loyalist forces were the underdog, the "little people," fighting not only the moneyed and decadent aristocrats and power of the Church, but the machines of the German, Italian, and Spanish militarists as well.

The result of Hemingway's commitment to the Republican cause was for a time political rather than literary. In addition to his newspaper dispatches and articles, he did much in the way of fund-raising to aid the Loyalists. He wrote the film-narration for a documentary, *The Spanish Earth,* and then a play, *The Fifth Column.* Not until the spring of 1939, when it became clear that the Loyalist cause was doomed, did Hemingway turn from propaganda and journalism to begin *For Whom the Bell Tolls.* It was published in October 1940.

The result was a storm of controversy. Left-wing critics accused him of betraying the Republican cause; right-wing critics denounced him for offering a "hero" who seemed willing to work with Communists even while aware of their treachery; and liberal critics tended to praise him for political rather than literary reasons, as though he had written a treatise instead of a novel. But Ernest Hemingway could not be placed neatly in a political pigeonhole, and neither could *A Farewell to Arms.*

"NO MAN IS AN ILAND." Perhaps one reason for the difficulty is that far more than a study of politics, *For Whom the Bell Tolls* is a study of the individual involved in what was a very political war. But it differs greatly from Hemingway's earlier studies of the individual hero in the world, because in this book the hero accepts his community, not merely with other members of a heroic elect, but with all of mankind, and chooses the nature of his personal confrontation with death accordingly. The nature of this community is stated with great beauty in the quotation from one of the poet John Donne's sermons upon the death of a close friend, the quotation from which the book takes its title:

> No man is an Iland, intire of it selfe; every man is a peece of the Continent, a part of the maine; if a Clod bee washed away by the Sea, Europe is the less, as well as if a Promontorie were, as well as if a Mannor of thy friends or of thine own were; any mans death diminishes me, because I am involved in Mankinde; And therefore never send to know for whom the bell tolls; It tolls for thee.

Thus, while the individual hero retains the sterling qualities of the Hemingway Code, he has been enlarged by what we might term his reunion with mankind. In the end, he finds the world a "fine place," that is "worth fighting for." In his personal confrontation with death, Robert Jordan realizes that there is a larger cause that man can choose to serve—in this he differs from the earlier Hemingway hero. The insistence that his action and its form be a matter of individual will is still there, along with the need to ritualize and dominate that action However, the issue is no longer a single matador against a single bull, or the single individual against a mass environment, but the individual who is *at the same time* the "instrument" of mankind against an essentially anti-human, machine-allied power. If Hemingway and his hero are on anyone's side, it is on the side of the human being. The political issues in the book are therefore seen, not as a contrast of black and white, but in the shaded tones of reality.

THE HERO'S DRIVE TO ACTION. But while Jordan is the epitome of the hero in his actions—he is in command of himself and his circumstances to a far greater extent than Hemingway's previous heroes—he is driven to confront reality by deep emotional needs. Jordan's drives in the novel seem to be a direct reflection of Hemingway's own, for Hemingway had also been deeply affected by the suicide of his own father. Suicide as an escape from reality represents a complete breach of the author's code, and the self-doubt and fear of futility which such an act instills in the children of individuals who commit suicide is a well-known psychological consequence. It is perhaps, therefore, the painfulness of their fears that makes Hemingway's heroes avoid "thinking" at all costs. For "thinking" too much may—as it did for Shakespeare's Hamlet—make "doing" impossible, and without something to act upon, something to do, the hero must face his inner sense of futility.

The fact that Jordan's basic motivations are emotional rather than political makes him an enigmatic figure to his compatriots, setting him apart from both the Spanish peasants whose cause he espouses, and the Communists who use the war itself for their own ideological ends. And in fact Hemingway himself seems to question the validity of Jordan's stance, both by forcing Jordan to question himself and by setting beside him very different and yet valid attitudes toward Jordan's ends in the persons of Pablo and Anselmo. As a character, Pablo certainly embodies such anti-heroic qualities as acceptance of defeat, lack of self-assertion, deviousness, and submission to domination by women. Yet through him Hemingway sets the idea of a concern for the life of one's immediate neighbor against Jordan's willingness to sacrifice his compatriots as well as himself for a larger mankind. Anselmo is Pablo's antithesis, typifying the hero as peasant farmer with all his qualities of toughness, self-reliance, gentleness, as well as the ability to act in a manly way. Through him Hemingway sets the question of whether killing can ever be justified against Jordan's insistence that in the right cause, the killing of men and animals is the same. The problem as a general one is not in the book, but the reader can see from the book itself that its complexity virtually precludes a tidy solution.

THE HEROINE AND THE AFFAIR. Jordan's relationship to Maria has been seen by many critics as representing merely an alternate to action, as an outlet for the hero's need to dominate when he cannot do so in action. But this does not appear to be the case: from the novel it seems that Jordan's passion for Maria runs deep and extends into his desires for the future. What is important to note is that in this relationship Jordan embodies the ideal of the hero in love who is yet free of woman; the hero whose love, unlike Frederic Henry's, is not a refuge but a source of strength which does not compromise his ability to act fully in the field of his choice.

Maria herself has been viewed, like Catherine in *A Farewell to Arms,* as too good to be true. In part this is due to the fact that many of those critics have judged her by the standards of American womanhood, to which she does not belong. In part her "goodness" can be seen as the natural behavior of a woman in love under the pressures of time and special circumstances. And the love affair of Jordan and Maria must be evaluated, as the critic Stewart Saunderson puts it, in terms of "the reader's own experience and belief, which will depend to some considerable extent on the values of the society in which he lives. If the reader has known that total communion of thought and emotion and body, that ecstasy in which 'one and one is one,' as Hemingway plainly puts it, what happens between Jordan and Maria is acceptable; if not, there is little to be said, except that Hemingway is by no means alone in believing such an experience to be possible."

MARIA AND PILAR. In her own person, Marie typifies the "good" all-woman type of heroine we have discussed above, with overtones of a pagan Aphrodite, the love goddess. In Maria, Hemingway has again created a heroine who has been tempered by personal tragedy, but he has also made her a symbol of all that is good but helpless before the power of organized evil. By contrast the character of Pilar embodies the elements of Hemingway's darker heroines who dominate men, but she shares with Brett Ashley the fact that she is not "bad." Like Brett, she is deeply involved in the concerns of men and is therefore not entirely feminine. Still, in Pilar we find those pagan attributes which identify the Hemingway woman, but we see her more as a primitive kind of earth mother than as a heavenly deity.

The images of mountain and plain are implicit rather than explicit in the book, but they carry the same import that they did in the previous novels. The action, and particularly Jordan's action, takes place in the mountains—an environment free from the mass warfare which offers the individual no chance to affirm himself through acts of courage, will, and choice. The warfare that is antithetical to the hero is waged on the plains, and it is from the plains that its danger penetrates Jordan's position in the hills.

REVIEW QUESTIONS: *FOR WHOM THE BELL TOLLS*

1. "Pure" is one of Hemingway's favorite words. Relate "purity" to his attitudes toward ideals and war as these are expressed in *For Whom the Bell Tolls*.

ANSWER: For Hemingway, action must be its own reward. Virtue, in other words, cannot be reconciled with self-interest, and for this reason Hemingway shows disdain for all those for whom the war represents a method of achieving some personal advantage. The professional soldier fights for a pay check, the professional politician for power, and the peasant for either a larger slice of the economic pie or revenge. For Hemingway, however, "pure" action exists by and for itself. He expresses this attitude through Robert Jordan's admiration for the volunteers of the International brigade whose motives are "puritanical" and "religious," and his disgust with the politicians at Gaylords, whose motives are a matter of self-interest.

2. Pablo has been called "an extremely complicated man and not altogether a villain." Discuss the significance of such a character in Hemingway's work.

ANSWER: One of the characteristics of Hemingway's ideal hero is his directness and simplicity and his conscious concern with finding simplicity in life. The fact that Hemingway creates a character who is the hero's antithesis in this respect and is yet "not altogether a villain" indicates that the author has made room for a larger view of life, even within the carefully selected kind of life that we see in his novels. It indicates that Hemingway was considering the possibility that such expedient, immediate goals as preserving the lives of those people who have become one's personal responsibility may have validity even in the face of such "pure" goals as preserving mankind. The fact that Pablo is not altogether bad also raises the question of whether anger and necessity as motives for killing may not have a validity which questions Jordan's cold and "surgical" detachment in action. In Pablo, Hemingway has drawn a many faceted portrait of good and evil, weakness and strength, brutality and gentleness that emerges as one of the most human representations in the book.

3. Compare the narrative technique of *For Whom the Bell Tolls* with Hemingway's earlier work.

ANSWER: Hemingway's earlier novels were narrated in the first-person and enclosed within a single point of view, but *For Whom the Bell Tolls* uses several different narrative techniques. There are internal monologues (where the reader is "in the mind" of a particular character), objective descriptions ("seen" or "heard" by the author rather than by any specific character), rapid shifts of point of view, and in general a looser structure than Hemingway used for books such as *A Farewell to Arms* or *The Sun Also Rises*. This was made necessary by the fact that *For Whom the Bell Tolls* is more ambitious in scope than Hemingway's earlier books. It attempts to render not merely an isolated though representative fragment of a conflict, but to reflect the very nature of the political, philosophical, and economic struggles which made the Spanish Civil War so complex.

IV. THE OLD MAN AND THE SEA

For Ernest Hemingway, far more than for most men, the spectre of age was a terrible spectre indeed; the virtue of action upon which he had based his art and his life was the virtue of the young. Even in his later years Hemingway was delightfully "boyish" (or regrettably so, depending on one's point of view); the problem of age was never far from his mind nor, for that matter, from his conversation—and in this connection Lillian Ross' *New Yorker* piece on Hemingway (May 13, 1950) is of particular interest.

AN APPROACH TO AGE. Whether Hemingway ever achieved an ultimate solution to this dilemma is not for us to judge, although the circumstances of his death would indicate that he could not and would not abide a final weakening of those powers which were so important to the protagonists of his stories. In the last decade or so of his life, however, Hemingway did find a way to cope with the fact of his own age: he would dramatize what he could not avoid. "Because of his absolute youthfulness," prophetically remarked one of his closest friends, "he regards old-growing as an utter and complete tragedy, as it is of course, the only true tragedy, and he is not going to degrade himself by maturing or anything absurd of that sort. All the same, since he has a sense of costume, he will emphasize his decline in all its hopelessness by sprouting a white beard and generally acting the part of *senex*."

If the young Hemingway had been an almost legendary figure of youthful and virile adventure, the old Hemingway would take up the role of Grand Old Man, the battle-scarred veteran, the aging but still indomitable combatant. Hemingway "The Champ," in other words (as he liked to call himself), would become "Papa" Hemingway—the Citizen of the World still rough-edged and manfully poetic, but mellowed by experience and years, and come to full bloom as a connoisseur of life, bullfighters, women, fishing, and war.

THE WISDOM OF HUMILITY. The resources of age rather than the powers of youth would henceforth be Hemingway's public role, and this was to provide the substance of his literary role as well. For *The Old Man and the Sea,* published in 1952, is the story not of youthful idealism, or youthful love in a world of chaos, or youthful frustration and anguish (bolstered by a code of manly non-sentiment), but rather the story of an aged "champion" for whom the power of will has replaced the power of flesh, and the wisdom of humility has replaced the arrogance of either simple pessimism or romantic self-sacrifice.

Old but not senile, "unlucky" but not defeated, gentle but not soft, proud but not boastful, resigned but not passive, and—perhaps most important—hopeful for himself without being jealous of others, Santiago the fisherman is himself a poet of the human spirit. He may "symbolize" the artist who attempts the impossible by going "too far out"; he may represent the Christ-like essence of willed suffering; or he may speak to us of the love and sharing which permeates all life—not just human life—despite its tragedy, isolation, and ultimate death. Whatever meaning is the "true" meaning of Santiago (and they can all be true), the quality of *The Old Man of the Sea* is that of poetry rather than prose. In the music of its language, the simplicity of its "story," and the indefinable essence of its dignity, this may well be the finest book Ernest Hemingway wrote.

SYMBOLISM. "No good book was ever written that had symbols arrived at beforehand and stuck in," said Hemingway, with characteristic bluntness. What he did not deny, however, was that action and event, objects and landscapes could be both literal and symbolic; that "facts" themselves could "mean" more than the simple reality of their own existence. When Hemingway describes the true as opposed to the false bull-fighter, for example, he is also presenting us with his own aesthetic creed as a writer: the same qualities which create "truth" for the one, create truth and beauty for the other. But the first requirement is that the description of the bullfight itself be accurate and real, and that no "meaning" be superimposed on the subject at the cost of real experience and real life.

To say that *The Old Man and the Sea* is a work of literary symbolism, however, is not to deny the importance of its story; in fact, it is the way that the story is put together that creates the symbolism. This is also true of the other Hemingway novels we have considered, novels in which people, landscapes and action exist on a particular and "real" level, but which create a deeper reality than would be obvious from the surface of the plot.

What is different about *The Old Man and the Sea* is not that it represents any sharp departure in Hemingway's literary style or personal philosophy, but rather that in this small book the style and philosophy seem to be in perfect equilibrium. There are no loose ends of narrative, episode, or motivation, and in this sense the book has been justly compared to a lyric poem. It also gives us, in a most lucid and economical form, the personal vision of Ernest Hemingway—a vision that accepts the fact of man's ultimate destruction, but insists that even in that destruction man need not accept defeat but can achieve a spiritual victory.

The means to spiritual victory for Hemingway have always been embodied in the Code, and it is essentially this Code to which the fisherman Santiago adheres. In keeping with the heroic ideal, he is unflinching in his confrontation with things as they are; courageous in action; without self-pity in pain; and views the world and its creatures without self-righteousness.

A CHANGE IN QUALITY. But for Santiago the Code has undergone subtle changes in meaning which change the *quality* of the hero in a profound way. Hemingway's original hero held that there was no God, no human nature; the older, wiser hero is clearly aware of a power beyond himself and beyond what he perceives. But while he acknowledges that it exists he does not view it as either demanding or benevolent; instead he sees that such a power is not active: rather it is a presence before which all creatures of the earth are equal. Thus there is no way in which the hero can call on its power for his own ends, and like the original hero he must acknowledge that whatever he is or does he must become or accomplish by himself. His success in his ventures will come only from luck and skill— for the hero still believes in luck. His skill, which consists of his knowledge of and conformance to the ritual prescribed for the action he has undertaken, is also a virtue of the original hero.

Another change which follows upon the recognition of the nature of this power in the world is that the hero is no longer alone. In recognizing the equality of all creatures before this power, he finds himself in a community of peers, in which all are in a sense his brothers. This is very different in effect from the equality which the original hero used to establish the unjustifiability of self-pity; in that context all creatures were equal in that they were "biologically" trapped, but they remained separate in their anguish in the world. We saw, of course, that Hemingway had taken a giant step toward this new conclusion in *For Whom the Bell Tolls,* where the hero accepted the fact that he was involved in mankind. But now the hero is not merely *involved* in the world of men; he is *related* to them, and even further, to all the creatures of the earth.

The close relationship between Santiago and the non-human as well as the human world is essential to the power of the novel. For the hero is exposed to the possibility of destruction at every moment of his long struggle; the hunter, in short, may at any moment become the hunted. But because of this relationship, because the marlin assumes the very proportions of Santiago himself, the struggle assumes the proportions of a heroic combat whose outcome is of the greatest importance to us.

But as we are aware, it is not the actual outcome that is so vital but the way it is achieved; whether the hero will yield to fear and give up the struggle, by giving up in fact or by falling back on self-pity or by appealing to a divine power. The triumph of Santiago is that he does not yield, even as the fish triumphs as it fights until he is overmastered. In fact, even as he is brought to the brink of physical death, Santiago seems to grow in insight and understanding of his circumstances, and returns from his trip beyond the pale no sadder, but wiser.

The new hero's wisdom and understanding also differs subtly from his earlier type—compassion has replaced the old "irony and pity." The ideal of irony and pity which found particular expression in *The Sun Also Rises* presumes a kind of lofty position for the hero from which he looks down upon those who do not belong to the club of the elect. But compassion implies love, and thus we can see that this difference also grows out of the recognition of an impartial power in the world, for with the brotherhood of all creatures, love for all is possible.

CHRIST AND ARTIST. The basic symbolism of the novel has been viewed by its critics primarily in two ways. Both can be helpful, and they can, in fact, be related to each other. The first approach views the story as an allegory of the artist at work, and particularly of Hemingway and his creation and reception of *Across the River and Into the Trees*. The book, as Sanderson views it, "was a work of stock-taking and reassessment, in which he experimented with new devices for projecting the emotional content of his characters . . . He was (at his best) only sporadically, and the result is disappointingly uneven." Other critics were less kind.

If we view this book as an allegory of the artist at work we may interpret the symbolism in the following manner. There is the setting out alone into the sea of the unconscious, and the careful setting of mental "bait" at various levels of the deep inner self. There is the care that must be taken that the "bait," the initial ideas, are set and kept at the right depth, or one may find that what one assumes to be a profound "catch" is only something from the surface levels of the mind. There is the "hooking" of the basic idea from the depth, and the long struggle of bringing it up into its final form as a work of art and making it one's own. And finally there is the return in which the critics attack the work, tearing at it voraciously with their analyses, until for the artist, there is nothing left but the skeleton of his original idea to show the grandeur of his original intent. What was Hemingways conclusion in this context? One may assume that in terms of the story, he had gone out too far.

The second approach to the novel, which finds considerable support, views *The Old Man and the Sea* as a loosely woven allegory of the last days of Christ. From this point of view, Christ and Santiago are both fishermen and moral teachers. Santiago's forty days of bad luck can be viewed as parallel to Christ's forty days on the mountain. Further, he suffers in his struggle with the fish for three days, as Christ suffered three days on the cross. Santiago's hands are torn as Christ's were pierced by nails, his back is lashed by the line as Christ's was lashed before being taken to Calvary, and he gets a piercing headache, as Christ was subjected to pain by the crown of thorns. Still further, Santiago kills the fish at noon on the third day, as the soldier pierced Christ's side with a spear at noon on His third day on the cross. Finally, Santiago carries his mast, as Christ carried His cross, and Santiago finally falls upon his bed in the attitude of Christ on the cross.

The transfer of the Christ image from Santiago to the fish at the moment of death can be understood in at least two ways.

First, the fish has always been a symbol of Christ in the Christian religion and is identified with Him, so that Christ, fish and fisherman are, in a sense, one. Secondly, the ritual of the Roman Catholic Mass includes a moment—the moment of Transubstantiation—when the priest is made one with Christ, as the priest-fisherman is united with the Christ-fish. In any case, Hemingway underlines this momentary union of fisherman and fish in the novel. It is a phenomenon which the reader will also remember from *The Sun Also Rises,* where the matador becomes one with the bull at the moment that he kills it.

But if the analogy of Santiago and Christ is accepted—as the specific elements of the novel suggest that it must be—it is also necessary to conclude that Santiago represents Christ as a man who has been perfected by his inner struggle and courage rather than Christ as a preordained deity. To those for whom the ethic of Christ as God has been cheapened by abuse and empty rhetoric, the ethic of Christ as a recognizable man of our own time can have new meaning even if the names are the same. The critic Clinton Burhans has the importance of this aspect of the novel clear:

> . . . out of (his) concern with action and conduct in a naturalistic universe, Hemingway has not evolved new moral values; rather, he has reaffirmed man's oldest ones —courage, love, humility, solidarity, and interdependence. It is their basis which is new—a basis not in supernaturalism or abstraction but hard-won through actual experience in a naturalistic universe which is at best indifferent to man and his values . . . Through perfectly realized symbolism and irony, then, Hemingway has beautifully and movingly spun out of an old fisherman's great trial . . . a pragmatic ethic and its basis in an essentially tragic vision of man; and in this reaffirmation of man's most cherished values and their reaffirmation in the terms

of our time rests the deepest and the enduring significance of *The Old Man and the Sea*.

REVIEW QUESTIONS: *THE OLD MAN AND THE SEA*

1. How does *The Old Man and the Sea* exemplify the "Hemingway Code"?

ANSWER: The "Hemingway Code" of manhood does not involve mere physical strength, sexual potency, or an ability to accumulate (or spend) wealth. According to this code, a man is defined by will, pride, and endurance: the endurance to accept pain, even loss—when the loss cannot be avoided; the pride of knowing that one has done one's best, and has acted according to one's own nature; and the will to face both defeat and victory truly, without whining on the one hand or boasting of the other.

Santiago the fisherman certainly does embody this code, which is essentially one of human dignity rather than "success" of any sort. Santiago, despite his age and poverty is a "man" in the fullest sense of the word. Although his strength has gone, his endurance and will remain; faced with defeat, he does not quit. He is undefeated.

2. Discuss *The Old Man and the Sea* as a work of literary symbolism.

ANSWER: Literary symbolism is a method which organizes the "facts" of real life and real experience, so that the facts themselves "mean" more than their own existence on a literal level. Symbolic meaning, however, must arise naturally from the facts, rather than be superimposed upon them. Symbolism, in short, might be described as "reality-plus"—a way of writing in which the "facts" of a story are quite true-to-life, but somehow "echo in the mind" with significance beyond that of the story itself. In this sense, then, *The Old Man and the Sea* is a work of literary symbolism. For the story of Santiago is very "real" indeed; Hemingway writes with his usual care and precision to achieve an exact portrait of "the way it was" in real life; every detail of fishing, of action, is clearly recreated. Over and above this reality—or perhaps one might say permeating it—is an "echo" of additional meaning. Christian symbolism, for example, runs throughout the book: the parallel to the suffering and nobility of Jesus (who was also a "fisherman") is obvious.

This is not to say that Santiago himself is necessarily a Christ figure. For the Crucifixion itself is a symbol of willed sacrifice, of the power and beauty of the human spirit, and other interpretations of *The Old Man and the Sea* are quite possible; indeed, more than one meaning might be "right"—and this too is characteristic of literary symbolism. Some critics, for example, have seen the book as symbolizing the pain, suffering, loneliness, and glory of the artist who does what every true artist must do: that is, attempt to go "too far out." Even the scavenger-sharks may be seen as symbolizing those who are defined merely by their own appetite, or those who feed on the artist's agony and endurance. The essential point is that *The Old Man and the Sea* does have these "echoes" of meaning which transcend the "facts" of the story—although the facts themselves are beautiful and realistically described.

3. On what basis does Santiago associate himself with the great DiMaggio?

ANSWER: Santiago sees in Joe DiMaggio, the great baseball player, much of his own pride, will, and endurance. Like Santiago himself, DiMaggio is no longer the great champion he was; the baseball hero suffers, moreover, from much pain because of a bone spur on his heel. DiMaggio, however, continues to "play the game," using his skill, his "heart," and his endurance to replace his early strength. And this is why Santiago associates himself with the ballplayer.

SURVEY OF CRITICAL OPINION OF ERNEST HEMINGWAY

That Ernest Hemingway is indeed one of the major figures of American literature is indicated by the fact that in sheer bulk there is more writing about his work than Hemingway himself ever produced. The stream of Hemingway criticism has been continuous and enormous, and gives no sign of drying up. Critics not only in the English-speaking countries, but in virtually every Continental country as well—not to mention many in the Orient—have examined Hemingway's work. Such international critical attention is perhaps even more significant than the Nobel Prize awarded to Hemingway in 1954.

This is not to say that critical opinion on Ernest Hemingway is in any sense unanimous. Although foreign critics have tended to be enthusiastic about Hemingway's work, they have also tended to view it in broadly cultural rather than strictly aesthetic terms, seeing in his writing a reflection of that violence which is so close to the surface of the "American character." With the exception of a few Spanish critics such as Arturo Barea, who insist that Hemingway was trapped by his own preoccupations even (or especially) when dealing with other cultures, there seems among foreign critics to be a certain fascination with Hemingway the man rather than Hemingway the artist, and the result has tended to be sociological and psychological rather than literary analysis.

HEMINGWAY ON HIS CRITICS. English and American critics, of course, have not been altogether free from the "Hemingway image"; from the very beginning, much critical ammunition has been expended on Hemingway's life and personal philosophy, rather than on the art for which this philosophy provided the raw material. Hemingway himself was often impatient, to put it mildly, with those "schoolmarm" critics who insisted on rapping his knuckles for Moral Reasons instead of looking at his books as books. In 1929, for example, Hemingway wrote a "Valentine" to critics:

> Sing a song of critics
> pockets full of lye
> four and twenty critics
> hope that you will die
> hope that you will peter out
> hope that you will fail
> so they can be the first one
> be the first to hail
> any happy weakening or sign of quick decay.
> (All very much alike, weariness to great,
> sordid small catastrophes, stack the cards on fate,
> very vulgar people, annals of the callous,
> dope fiends, soldiers, prostitutes,
> men without a gallus) . . . .
> (From *Little Review* 12, May, 1929, p. 42)

NEGATIVE CRITICISM. Not all the depreciatory criticism, however, was the work of "schoolmarm" critics; from Sean O'Faolain to Leon Edel, from Wyndham Lewis to Harry Levin, critics and creative writers attacked what they viewed as an extremely "thin" art, an art whose protagonists could only deal with complexity by running away from it, by taking refuge in mindless action—action in which killing men was put on the same level as shooting animals, and shooting animals was put on the same level as making love to women, and making love to women was put on the same level as drinking wine.

Hemingway's art, in short, was seen as an art of "evasion" rather than confrontation; anything which the Hemingway hero could not reduce to a sort of appendage to his own ego, the critics insisted, was simply eliminated from any consideration whatsoever, and the result was an art based less on economy of style than on failure of imagination; by eliminating all that he could not fit into his private ritual, Hemingway produced books of the mindless for the mindless, books which (despite a certain narrative skill and ease in reading) reduced human motivations to an adolescent formula, and human love to an auto-erotic image. If the Hemingway woman was, as Edmund Wilson once remarked, "amoeba-like," the Hemingway man was hardly more impressive—except, of course, when shooting something, or drinking something, or going to bed with one of the "amoebas." Perhaps one might sum up the "anti-Hemingway" school of criticism in the following phrase: "He was the best 17-year-old novelist who ever lived."

AFFIRMATIVE CRITICISM. Those critics who see Hemingway as a major artist, however—and their number is legion—insist that Hemingway's work is "simple" only on the surface; that his heroes are neither callous nor mindless, but possessed of enormous sensitivity both to human dishonesty and universal suffering; that his style communicates far more than it overtly states; and that in his best books Ernest Hemingway is a lyric poet of the English language. Such critics remind us that for Ernest Hemingway the "real" world is itself an arena where the human soul must struggle to face its own mortality, and that if he did limit his subject matter, he did so deliberately, in order to achieve an essentially formal rather than "realistic" art.

That Hemingway is capable of complete realism, is indicated by those scenes which he chooses to render with breath-taking precision; that he has deliberately limited his subject matter to particular types and situations is hardly unique with Hemingway. From workers in stone such as the Greek architects, to workers in words such as the American novelist Henry James, creative artists have always limited their subject matter, and have so utilized it that the subject transcends its own limitations. The subject or material which an artist uses is less important than the universality he achieves, and in this respect, as Carlos Baker has pointed out, Hemingway is perhaps this country's most universal writer; his work has been translated in all parts of the world, and speaks to the essential humanity of individual human beings of all cultures and all races.

THE STATURE OF HEMINGWAY. Ernest Hemingway, indeed, may well have been more sophisticated than many of his critics. He read much, and was deeply aware of literary development and history. If he distrusted over-embellishment, and insisted (as he remarked in *Death in the Afternoon*) that the Age of the Baroque is over, such a conviction is as legitimate as any other for the working artist, who after all must develop his own style and his own craft to the point where it will serve as an instrument for his particular vision of human destiny. And the Hemingway vision is, despite the violence of his subject matter, an affirmative one: in a period when annihilation hangs like a sword of Damocles over Western Civilization, Hemingway offers the hope of individual value. His "code," as Mark Spilka has pointed out, "gives meaning to a world where love and religion are defunct, where the proofs of manhood are difficult and scarce, and where every man must learn to define his own moral conditions and then live up to them."

Whether for praise or blame, Hemingway's critics have agreed upon one thing: that he is one of the great figures of our time. Almost a legend in his own lifetime, Hemingway was a remarkable man as well as a remarkable writer. It remains to be seen, of course, whether his books will survive for very long after his death, but in this matter each reader must judge for himself.

BIBLIOGRAPHICAL SUGGESTIONS AND STUDY GUIDE

GENERAL BACKGROUND.

Callaghan, Morley, *That Summer in Paris,* New York, 1963.
Cowley, Malcolm, *Exile's Return,* New York, 1961.
Loeb, Harold, *The Way it Was,* New York, 1959.
Orwell, George, *Homage to Catalonia,* Boston, 1955.
Reade, James Morgan, *Atrocity Propaganda,* New Haven, 1941.
Stallings, Lawrence, *The First World War,* New York, 1933.
Stein, Gertrude, *The Autobiography of Alice B. Toklas,* New York, 1933.
Thomas, Hugh, *The Spanish Civil War,* New York, 1961.
Tuchman, Barbara W., *The Guns of August,* New York, 1962.
Wheelock, John Hall, ed. *Editor to Author: The Letters of Maxwell Perkins,* New York, 1950.

CRITICISM AND LITERARY HISTORY.

For a checklist of Hemingway criticism to 1955 see the Hemingway number of *Modern Fiction Studies,* Volume I, Number 3, 1955. For the period from 1955 to 1961 see "A Checklist of Hemingway Criticism," *Hemingway and his Critics,* ed. Carlos Baker, New York, 1961. The attention of the student is drawn to the fact that articles in periodicals are an extremely useful and perhaps major source of Hemingway criticism. Both checklists noted above give excellent selections of such periodical essays, and also list criticism on individual works. The following books are also useful, especially the anthologies of critical articles edited by Baker and Weeks:

Atkins, John Alfred, *The Art of Ernest Hemingway,* London, 1952.

Baker, Carlos, *Hemingway: The Writer as Artist,* Princeton, 1952.
Baker, Carlos, ed., *Hemingway and his Critics,* New York, 1961 (an anthology of critical articles).
Baker, Carlos, ed., *Ernest Hemingway: Critiques of Four Major Novels,* New York, 1962 (an anthology of critical articles).
Beach, Joseph Warren, *American Fiction,* 1920-1940, New York, 1941.
Bishop, John Peale, *Collected Essays of John Peale Bishop,* ed. Edmund Wilson, New York, 1948.
Burgum, Edwin Berry, *The Novel and the World's Dilemma,* New York, 1947.
Cohn, Louis H., *A Bibliography of the Works of Ernest Hemingway,* New York, 1931.
Daiches, David, *The Novel and the Modern World,* New York, 1940.
Fenton, Charles A., *The Apprenticeship of Ernest Hemingway,* New York, 1954.
Fiedler, Leslie A., *Love and Death in the American Novel,* Cleveland, 1962.
Frohock, W. M., *The Novel of Violence in America,* Dallas, 1958.
Geismar, Maxwell, *Writers in Crisis: The American Novel Between Two Wars,* Boston, 1942.
Hoffman, Frederick J., *The Modern Novel in America,* 1900-1950, Chicago, 1951.
Hoffman, Frederick J., *The Twenties: American Writing in the Postwar Decade,* New York, 1955.
Kazin, Alfred, *On Native Grounds,* New York, 1942.
McCaffery, John K. M., ed., *Ernest Hemingway, the Man and his Work,* Cleveland, 1950.
Muller, Herbert J., *Modern Fiction: A Study in Values,* New York, 1937.
Poore, Charles, ed., *The Hemingway Reader,* New York, 1953.
Savage, D. S., *The Withered Branch: Six Studies in the Modern Novel,* London, 1950.

Snell, George, *The Shapers of American Fiction*, New York, 1947.

Thorp, Willard, *American Writing in the Twentieth Century*, Cambridge, 1960.

Wagenknecht, Edward, *Cavalcade of the American Novel*, New York, 1952.

West, Ray B., and R. W. Stallman, *The Art of Modern Fiction*, New York, 1949.

Wilson, Edmund, *The Wound and the Bow*, London, 1941.

Wilson, Edmund, *The Shores of Light*, New York, 1953.

Weeks, Robert P., ed., *Hemingway: A Collection of Critical Essays*, Englewood, 1962 (a very useful anthology of criticism).

Young, Philip, *Ernest Hemingway*, New York, 1952.

NOTES

NOTES

NOTES

NOTES

NOTES

NOTES

NOTES

MONARCH® NOTES AND STUDY GUIDES

ARE AVAILABLE AT RETAIL STORES EVERYWHERE

In the event your local bookseller cannot provide you with other Monarch titles you want—

ORDER ON THE FORM BELOW:

Complete order form appears on inside front & back covers for your convenience.

Simply send retail price, local sales tax, if any, plus 25¢ to cover mailing & handling.

IBM #	AUTHOR & TITLE (exactly as shown on title listing)	PRICE
	PLUS ADD'L FOR POSTAGE	25¢
	GRAND TOTAL	

MONARCH® PRESS, a division of Simon & Schuster, Inc.
Mail Service Department, 1 West 39th Street, New York, N.Y. 10018

I enclose _____ dollars to cover retail price, local sales tax, plus mailing and handling.

Name _____
(Please print)
Address _____
City _____ State _____ Zip _____

Please send check or money order. We cannot be responsible for cash.